D0786212

APR 2015

Your Guide to Government

What is the judicial branch?

Ellen Rodger

Crabtree Publishing Company

www.crabtreebooks.com

Crabtree Publishing Company

www.crabtreebooks.com

Author: Ellen Rodger
Coordinating editor: Kathy Middleton
Series editor: Valerie J. Weber
Editors: Valerie J. Weber, Lynn Peppas, Crystal Sikkens
Proofreaders: Sangeeta Gupta, Kelly McNiven
Discussion questions: Reagan Miller
Production coordinator: Ken Wright
Prepress technician: Ken Wright
Project manager: Summit Kumar (Q2A Bill Smith)
Art direction: Joita Das (Q2A Bill Smith)
Cover design: Samara Parent
Design: Roshan (Q2A Bill Smith)
Photo research: Ranjana Batra (Q2A Bill Smith)
Print coordinator: Katherine Berti

Written, developed, and produced by Q2A Bill Smith

Photographs:
Cover: 350z33/Wikimedia Commons (right), Steve Petteway, Collection of the Supreme Court of the United States/Wikimedia Commons (inset); Title page: Shutterstock;P4: S.Borisov/Shutterstock; P5: Konstantin L/Shutterstock; P6: dc_slim/Shutterstock; P7: monkeybusinessimages/ iStockphoto; P8: DEA Picture Library/De Agostini/Getty Images; P9: MPI/Stringer/Hulton Fine Art Collection/Getty Images; P10: Howard Chandler Christy; P11: National Archives of the Unites States; P12: pio3/Shutterstock; P13: Collection of the Supreme Court of the United States; P14: New York Daily News Archive/Getty Images; P15: The National Gallery of Art; P16: MCT/McClatchy-Tribune/Getty Images; P17: Bachrach/Getty Images; P18: Visions of America / Purestock/Glow Images; P19: Greg Mathieson/Mai/Time & Life Pictures/Getty Images; P20: Clarence Holmes Photography /Alamy; P21: Saul Loeb/AFP/Getty Images; P22: Joe Raedle/Getty Images News/Getty Images; P23: Radius Images/Glow Images; P24: Orlando Sentinel/McClatchy-Tribune/Getty Images; P25: Janet S. Robbins/Alamy; P26: Andrey Eremin/Shutterstock; P27: Tim Sloan/AFP/Getty Images; P28: Robert W. Kelley/Time & Life Pictures/Getty Images; P29: Paul Schutzer/Time & Life Pictures/Getty Images; P30: Pool/Getty Images News/Getty Images News; P31: Dan Kitwood/Getty Images News/Getty Images

Library and Archives Canada Cataloguing in Publication

Rodger, Ellen
    What is the judicial branch? / Ellen Rodger.

(Your guide to government)
Includes index.
Issued also in electronic formats.
ISBN 978-0-7787-0880-3 (bound).--ISBN 978-0-7787-0906-0 (pbk.)

    1. Courts--United States--Juvenile literature. 2. Law--United States--Juvenile literature. I. Title. II. Series: Your guide to government

KF8720.R63 2013   j347.73'1   C2013-900353-3

Library of Congress Cataloging-in-Publication Data

Rodger, Ellen.
    What is the judicial branch? / Ellen Rodger.
      pages cm. -- (Your guide to government)
    Includes index.
    ISBN 978-0-7787-0880-3 (reinforced library binding) -- ISBN 978-0-7787-0906-0 (pbk.) -- ISBN 978-1-4271-9313-1 (electronic pdf) -- ISBN 978-1-4271-9237-0 (electronic html)
    1. Courts--United States--Juvenile literature. 2. Procedure (Law)--United States--Juvenile literature. 3. Law--United States--Juvenile literature. I. Title.

KF8720.R63 2013
347.73'1--dc23
                        2013001275

Crabtree Publishing Company

www.crabtreebooks.com   1-800-387-7650

Printed in the U.S.A./092014/CG20140808

Published in Canada
Crabtree Publishing
616 Welland Ave.
St. Catharines, ON
L2M 5V6

Published in the United States
Crabtree Publishing
PMB 59051
350 Fifth Avenue, 59th Floor
New York, New York 10118

Published in the United Kingdom
Crabtree Publishing
Maritime House
Basin Road North, Hove
BN41 1WR

Published in Australia
Crabtree Publishing
3 Charles Street
Coburg North
VIC 3058

Contents

The Three Branches

Every country needs laws. Governments make, carry out, and enforce laws.

The United States federal government has three branches. They are the executive branch, the legislative branch, and the judicial branch. They have the power to make decisions about the country.

The president is the head of the executive branch. Presidents have many duties and powers. They direct the government and command the armed forces. They also approve or reject proposed laws.

The legislative branch includes the House of Representatives and the Senate. Together they form Congress. All members of Congress are elected. Congress makes laws.

The president lives in the White House in Washington, D.C. The executive branch of government often meets there.

The Supreme Court has been meeting in the Supreme Court building since 1935.

The Supreme Court heads the judicial branch. It is the country's highest court. Supreme Court judges review laws. They decide the meaning of the **Constitution**.

In Their Own Words

"We are under a Constitution, but the Constitution is what the judges say it is."
Charles Evans Hughes, New York governor and
11th Supreme Court Chief Justice, 1907

The Judicial Branch

The judicial branch deals with the laws of the country. It includes the U.S. Supreme Court and other courts. The judicial branch interprets, or explains, laws. It decides whether people have broken laws. If they have, it also decides what their punishment should be.

Laws are rules that people are supposed to follow. They protect people from being harmed by others. If people break laws, sometimes they go to jail or have to pay a fine. Without laws, a country could not run properly.

Several sculptures stand outside the Supreme Court building. This figure represents, or stands for, justice and law.

Imagine there were no laws about stealing. People could take what they wanted and you could do nothing about it. Laws have been created by Congress to prevent theft. People are less likely to steal knowing they can be punished.

Laws are also supposed to provide justice. Justice means fairness. People need to know that their government is treating them fairly.

Laws are meant to protect people. People who break laws are often punished.

In Their Own Words
"Injustice anywhere is a threat to justice everywhere."
Dr. Martin Luther King, Jr., civil rights leader, 1963

The Constitution

Britain lost the Revolutionary War (1775–1783). Here, a British general surrenders, or gives up, to an American general.

More than 200 years ago, America was still a group of colonies ruled by Great Britain. Britain passed laws that the colonists felt were unfair. The laws for America were made by a king and a government far away. The colonists **revolted**. They declared their independence in 1776.

After gaining their independence, Americans had to decide what kind of government they wanted. They wrote a constitution that would protect their freedom. The U.S. Constitution set up the different branches of government. It gave each branch separate powers. One branch could not be more powerful than another.

George Washington, Thomas Jefferson, and Alexander Hamilton discuss the country's Constitution. They were three of the founders of the United States.

The Constitution sets the rules for the government we have today. The Constitution was written more than 235 years ago! It is the oldest written constitution of any nation. It has been amended, or changed, many times.

WHAT DO YOU THINK?

If the Constitution was written 11 years after the colonists declared their independence, what year was it written in?

Working Together

The Constitution gives each branch of government its own duties. All branches must work together for the government to run. Congress has the power to propose laws. The president has the power to veto, or reject, laws passed by Congress. Congress can then override, or cancel, the president's veto.

The Supreme Court can override the decisions of both Congress and the president. It can tell Congress that a law Congress proposed goes against the Constitution. The Supreme Court can also tell presidents that they did something not allowed by the Constitution. This system is called checks and balances.

Leaders from different states decided what the new country's government would look like.

The Supreme Court building has a saying on its entrance. The words say, "EQUAL JUSTICE UNDER LAW." The court exists to treat all Americans fairly. It overturns laws that are against the Constitution. This process is called judicial review.

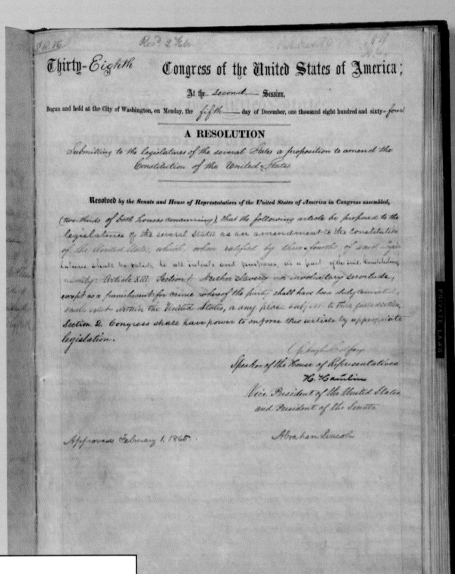

 The Constitution has been changed several times. These changes are called amendments. The 13th Amendment passed in 1865 outlawed slavery.

In Their Own Words

"The happy Union of these States is a wonder; their Constitution is a miracle; their example the hope of Liberty throughout the world."
James Madison, Founding Father and fourth president, 1829

The Supreme Court

The Supreme Court is the country's highest court. It was created by the Constitution in 1789. It hears 70 to 100 cases each year.

Most of the cases are **appeals** from lower courts. Appeals are requests to change the decisions of lower courts.

Thousands of appeal **petitions**, or requests, are made each year. The Supreme Court decides which petitions it will hear.

The Supreme Court has the final say in a court case. It is very hard to change a decision of the Supreme Court.

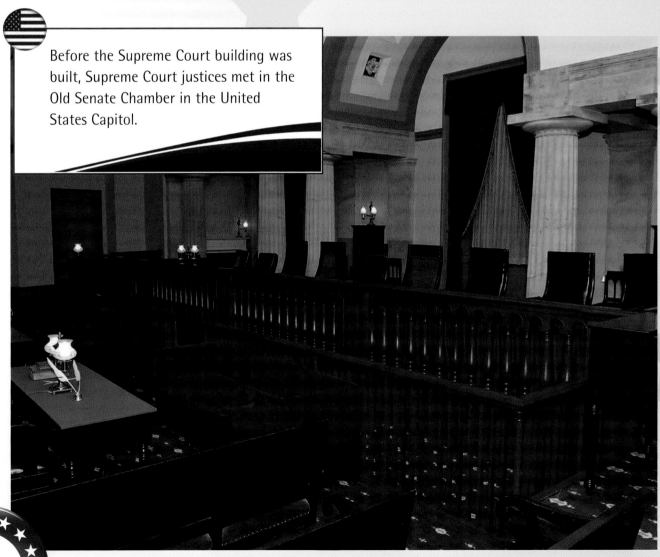

Before the Supreme Court building was built, Supreme Court justices met in the Old Senate Chamber in the United States Capitol.

Sonia Sotomayor is the Supreme Court's first Hispanic justice. She is also only the fourth female justice in the court's history. Justice Sotomayor wears a black robe when in court.

It is not easy to get a job on the Supreme Court. There are only nine judges, who are called justices. Supreme Court justices are nominated, or chosen, by the president. The Senate approves or rejects the president's choice.

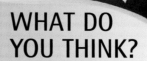

WHAT DO YOU THINK?

Who decides which cases are heard by the Supreme Court?

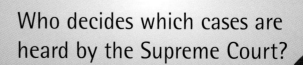

The Chief Justice

Imagine being the top judge of the highest court in the country! It is a difficult job with long hours.

The chief justice is the head of the judicial branch. The job has many duties. Some of them include:

- making sure the federal courts run properly
- representing the court
- swearing in presidents at the beginning of their term.

"I do solemnly swear . . ." Chief Justice John Roberts swore in President Barack Obama in 2009. Swearing in new presidents is just one of many jobs of the chief justice.

The chief justice of the United States is one of nine Supreme Court justices. These justices hold their jobs for life. Most leave after working about 15 years. Each justice, including the chief justice, has one vote in a decision.

The first chief justice was John Jay. Jay was a lawyer and a Founding Father of the United States. By 2012, there have been 17 chief justices.

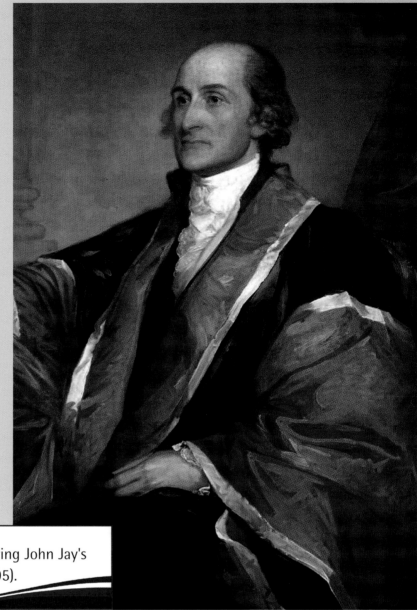

Only four cases were heard during John Jay's term as chief justice (1789–1795).

In Their Own Words

"When a president chooses a Supreme Court justice, he is placing in human hands the full authority and majesty of the law. The decisions of the Supreme Court affect the life of every American."
President George W. Bush, 2005

The Justices

Justices are the judges who make decisions. They are usually lawyers who know a lot about the law.

All Supreme Court justices are nominated by the president and approved by Congress. The justices of the Supreme Court serve for life, or until they retire or resign. They meet at the Supreme Court building in Washington D.C. This building contains a courtroom, justices' offices, and a court library. It even has a gym with a basketball court!

The Supreme Court's meetings begin on the first Monday of October. A meeting of the justices is called a session. Sessions run from October until June or July. Sometimes justices sit and hear cases. At other times, the court is in recess. When in recess, the justices think about cases and write their opinions. Opinions are **judgments** based on their ideas about the law.

The Supreme Court meets in this courtroom, called a chamber.

Thurgood Marshall was the first African American Supreme Court justice.

In Their Own Words

❝Law matters, because it keeps us safe, because it protects our most fundamental rights and freedoms, and because it is the foundation of our democracy.❞

Supreme Court Justice Elena Kagan, 2010

The Court System

The judicial branch of government is the federal court system. The word judicial means "judgment" or "justice." Courts hear cases and make judgments based on laws.

Besides the Supreme Court, the judicial branch also includes many lower federal courts. The main ones are the district courts and the courts of appeals.

Imagine the police thought you had robbed a federal bank. Your case may be heard in a district court. District courts are **trial courts**. A judge and a jury would decide if you were guilty or not. A jury is a small group of people chosen to hear the facts of a case.

The first Supreme Court meetings were held in Independence Hall in Philadelphia.

If you were found guilty, you would have the right to go to the United States Court of Appeals. Appeals are heard by three judges that work together on a case. You must submit a written report, called a brief, to the judges that shows the trial court made a legal error that affected your case. If the judges agree, they can overturn, or reverse, the trial court's decision.

The Court of Appeals usually has the final say, unless you submit a request to have the U.S. Supreme Court review your case. However, the Supreme Court only chooses to review about 100 cases a year. If the Supreme Court doesn't choose your case, the decision made by the Court of Appeals is final.

The United States Marshals Service is a federal police force. Marshals protect the courts and enforce federal laws.

District Courts

District courts are trial courts for the United States federal court system. Unlike the Supreme Court that was created by the Constitution, district courts were made by Congress. The district courts deal with cases where federal laws have been broken.

District courts also settle fights between people and companies. This area of the law is called civil law. Some U.S. district courts deal with special issues such as taxes.

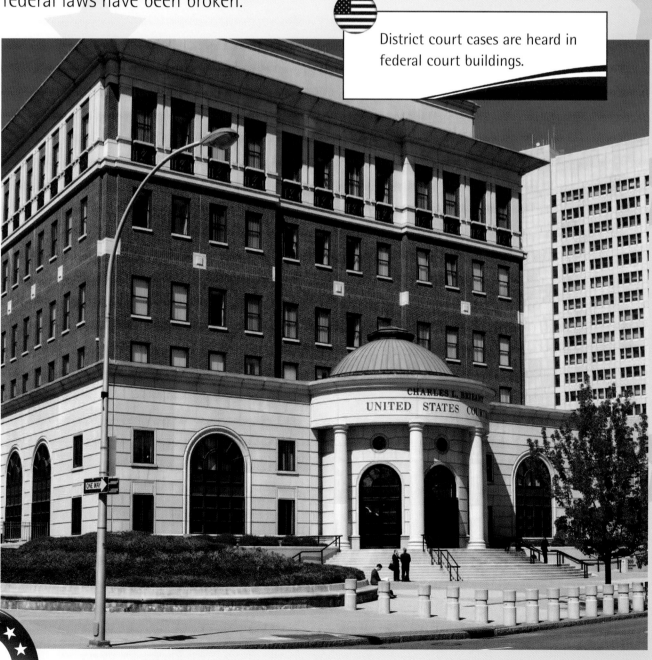

District court cases are heard in federal court buildings.

The United States is divided into judicial districts. Each district has one or more district courts. There are 89 districts within the 50 U.S. states, with at least one district court in each state. Cases in district courts are heard by a judge and jury. The district courts select U.S. citizens from the area to serve on a jury.

In March 2011, Judge Kimberly J. Mueller became the first female judge in the Eastern District Court of California.

WHAT DO YOU THINK?

What kinds of cases are heard in a district court?

Different U.S. Courts

There are many kinds of laws, including federal laws, state laws, and local laws. Different courts hear cases based on the laws that were broken. Federal courts are part of the judiciary branch. Each state sets up its own state courts to handle cases that involve state laws. Cities and counties have their own courts for local laws that are broken.

Jurisdiction is what makes these courts different from each other. When a law is broken, it must first be determined whether the law is a federal, state, or local law. That determines which court has the jurisdiction, or power, to hear and make a judgment on the case.

Federal courts hear cases about federal laws. They also hear cases where a state law goes against the Constitution. Because there are more state laws than any other kind, state courts have jurisdiction in most cases. Local courts hear cases that break city or county laws.

Local court officers bring a prisoner to court.

PRISONER

Federal courts can put federal bank robbers in jail for many years and make them pay a fine.

If you robbed a federal bank, your case would be heard in a federal district court. If you robbed a gas station, your case would be heard in a state court. If you wrote **graffiti** on a wall, your case may be heard in a local court.

Trials and Appeals

Trials take place in courts. In a trial, lawyers try to prove a **defendant** is guilty or innocent of a crime. A defendant is a person who may have done something against the law. Lawyers present **evidence**, or information, about what happened. A judge and jury decide a case.

If the defendant is found guilty, a judge decides the sentence. A sentence could mean time in prison or a fine.

Sometimes district courts make mistakes and innocent people are found guilty of crimes they did not commit. If a mistake was made, the U.S. federal court system allows defendants another chance.

A court reporter takes notes on a special machine during every trial. Sometimes a defendant asks for a new trial. The new court can then review these notes.

MAINE DISTRICT COURT

Some district court buildings look very different from the Supreme Court.

Defendants who are found guilty in district courts can appeal their case. They ask for another trial in the Court of Appeals. If they lose in the Court of Appeals, they can ask the Supreme Court to review their case. The Supreme Court reviews only some of these cases.

WHAT DO YOU THINK?

What happens if a mistake is made in a district court?

25

In Session

The Supreme Court meets in Washington, D.C., at the Supreme Court building. The justices gather in a courtroom. A court official yells, "hear ye," which is said as "oyez!" The court is then declared in session. The justices sit in tall black chairs and face the people in the court. The chief justice sits in the middle.

Lawyers then present their cases to the court. The justices listen. Sometimes several different cases are presented in one day. At the end of the day, the chief justice bangs a gavel. All the justices leave the courtroom.

The gavel is a symbol of a judge's power. Judges bang the gavel to start a trial or to stop people from being noisy.

The judges of the Supreme Court pose for a portrait in their official robes.

But that does not end their work. The justices study the case in their own chambers, or offices. Then they meet in another room. Each justice has one vote. Decisions are made by the majority of votes. Supreme Court decisions are final.

You and the Courts

Courts make many decisions. Some only affect the people involved. Others affect everyone. Some decisions made by federal courts have changed the way we all live in the United States.

In 1954, the Supreme Court overturned a state law that allowed **segregation**. Segregation means to set apart groups of people based on the color of their skin. The law allowed separate public schools for black students and white students. The Supreme Court said separate schools were unequal. According to the court, unequal schools were against the Constitution.

Separate schools and classrooms for black children were common before 1954.

Other places besides schools were also segregated. Some bus and train stations had separate waiting rooms. The Supreme Court's ruling changed the country.

This case was called Brown v. Board of Education. The letter v stands for versus, meaning "against." After the Supreme Court decision, white and black students started to go to the same schools. By 1968, the Supreme Court had declared that other laws that denied civil rights were also against the Constitution.

WHAT DO YOU THINK?

How did the Brown v. Board of Education case change schools today?

Other Countries' Courts

Every country has its own judicial branch and court systems. Each is based on the country's form of government and its traditions.

The Supreme Court of the United Kingdom is the country's highest court. It is the final appeals court. It has ten justices plus a president and deputy president.

Sometimes judges of the Supreme Court of Australia wear red robes and wigs.

Canada has a Supreme Court with nine justices appointed by the prime minister. The prime minister is the head of government. The Supreme Court of Canada is the country's highest court. It is also the final court of appeal.

The supreme court in France is called the Cour de Cassation, or Court of Cassation. It was established in 1790, during the **French Revolution**. It is the court of final appeal for civil and criminal cases.

Germany's supreme court is similar to the U.S. Supreme Court. It reviews laws to see if they are constitutional. But it does not normally hear appeals. Germany's government selects its judges.

British Supreme Court justices wear fancy robes for special events. Normally, they dress in business suits.

DISCUSSION QUESTIONS

1. At the entrance of the Supreme Court building, the following words are found: "EQUAL JUSTICE UNDER LAW." What do these words mean? How do they apply to the judicial branch?

2. Why is it difficult to take a case to the Supreme Court?

3. What laws and freedoms do you feel all people should have? Why?

Learning More

Books

Bedesky, Baron. *What Are the Levels of Government?* Crabtree Publishing, 2009.

Gorman, Jacqueline Laks. *Why Do We Have Laws?* Gareth Stevens Publishing, 2008.

Websites

Ben's Guide to U.S. Government for Kids: bensguide.gpo.gov/3-5/government/ national/ judicial.html

USA for Kids: www.usconsulate.org.hk/pas/kids/ judicial.htm

Glossary

appeals Requests to change a court's decision

Constitution A group of written laws that tell the government how it is to be run

defendant In a court of law, someone who has been accused of committing a crime

evidence The information or facts about something

French Revolution The overthrow of the French king in 1789 for a new system of government

graffiti Writing or drawing on a wall or other public surface that is against the law

judgments The decisions of a judge or court

petitions Formal requests for a change to something

revolted Rose up against or fought against a government

segregation The separation of people based on race

trial courts Courts where cases are first heard

Index